Born in 1997

by

Kerry Butters.

Born in 1997.

Millennium:	**2nd millennium**
Centuries:	19th century – **20th century** – 21st century
Decades:	1960s 1970s 1980s – **1990s** – 2000s 2010s 2020s
Years:	1994 1995 1996 – **1997** – 1998 1999 2000

1997 (MCMXCVII) was a common year starting on Wednesday (dominical letter E) of the Gregorian calendar, the 1997th year of the Common Era (CE) and *Anno Domini* (AD) designations, the 997th year of the 2nd millennium, the 97th year of the 20th century, and the 8th year of the 1990s decade.

Contents

Events

January

- January 17 – A Delta II rocket carrying a military GPS payload explodes, shortly after liftoff from Cape Canaveral.
- January 18 – In northwest Rwanda, Hutu militia members kill 6 Spanish aid workers, 3 soldiers, and seriously wound another.
- January 19 – Yasser Arafat returns to Hebron after more than 30 years, and joins celebrations over the handover of the last Israeli-controlled West Bank city.
- January 20 – U.S. President Bill Clinton is inaugurated for his second term.
- January 22 – Madeleine Albright becomes the first female Secretary of State, after confirmation by the United States Senate.
- January 23 – Mir Aimal Kasi is sentenced to death for a 1993 assault rifle attack outside CIA headquarters that killed 2 and wounded 3.

- January 27 – It is revealed that French museums had nearly 2,000 pieces of art that had been stolen by Nazis.
- January 31 - *Final Fantasy VII*, one of the most popular video games of all time, is released in Japan.

February

- February 4
    - On their way to Lebanon, 2 Israeli troop-transport helicopters collide, killing 73.
    - After at first contesting the results, Serbian President Slobodan Milošević recognizes opposition victories in the November 1996 elections.
    - British Home Secretary Michael Howard informs Moors Murderer Myra Hindley that she will never be released from prison. Mr. Howard has made the decision in agreement with a recommendation made by his predecessor David Waddington in 1990.
- February 5
    - The so-called "Big Three" banks in Switzerland announce the creation of a $71 million fund to aid Holocaust survivors and their families.
    - Morgan Stanley and Dean Witter Reynolds investment banks announce a $10 billion merger.
- February 10
    - The United States Army suspends Gene C. McKinney, Sergeant Major of the Army, its top-ranking enlisted soldier, after hearing allegations of sexual misconduct.

- Sandline affair: Australian newspapers publish stories that the government of Papua New Guinea has brought mercenaries onto Bougainville Island.
- February 13
  - *STS-82*: Tune-up and repair work on the Hubble Space Telescope is started by astronauts from the *Space Shuttle Discovery*.
  - The Dow Jones Industrial Average closes above 7,000 for the first time, gaining 60.81 to 7,022.44.
- February 22 – In Roslin, Scotland, scientists announce that an adult sheep named Dolly had been successfully cloned, and was born in July 1996.
- February 23 – A small fire occurs on the Russian space station Mir.
- February 27 – Divorce becomes legal in the Republic of Ireland.
- February 28 – North Hollywood shootout: Two robbers wearing kevlar body armor armed with AK-47s containing armor-piercing bullets injure 17 police officers and civilians in a gun battle. The incident sparks debate on the appropriate firepower for United States patrol officers to have available in similar situations in the future.

March

- March 4 – U.S. President Bill Clinton bans federal funding for any research on human cloning.
- March 6
  - Pablo Picasso's *Tête de Femme* is stolen from a London gallery (recovered a week later).

- In Sri Lanka, Tamil Tigers overrun a military base and kill more than 200.
- March 13
  - India's Missionaries of Charity chooses Sister Nirmala to succeed Mother Teresa as its leader.
  - The National People's Congress of the People's Republic of China creates a new Chongqing Municipality, out of part of Sichuan.
  - The Phoenix Lights, a series of UFOs, are seen over Phoenix, Arizona.
- March 16 – Sandline affair: On Bougainville Island, soldiers of commander Jerry Singirok arrest Tim Spicer and his mercenaries of the Sandline International.
- March 18 – The tail of a Russian An-24 charter plane breaks off while en route to Turkey, causing the plane to crash, killing all 50 on board, and resulting in the grounding of all An-24s.
- March 21
  - In Zaire, Etienne Tshiksekedi is appointed prime minister; he ejects supporters of Mobutu Sese Seko from his cabinet.
  - Mercenaries of Sandline International withdraw from Papua New Guinea.
- March 22
  - Tara Lipinski, 14, becomes the youngest women's world figure skating champion.
  - The Comet Hale–Bopp makes its closest approach to Earth.
- March 23 – The British detective drama show, *Midsomer Murders* broadcasts on ITV.

- March 24 – The 69th Academy Awards, hosted by Billy Crystal, are held at the Shrine Auditorium in Los Angeles, with *The English Patient* winning Best Picture.
- March 26
  - In San Diego, 39 Heaven's Gate cultists commit mass suicide at their compound.
  - Julius Chan resigns as prime minister of Papua New Guinea, ending the Sandline affair.
- March 31 - *Teletubbies* makes its debut on BBC2.

April

- April 1
  - Comet Hale–Bopp meets or exceeds most predictions when it passes perihelion.
  - The popular television series (based on the video games of the same name), Pokémon premieres on TV Tokyo.
- April 3 – The Thalit massacre in Algeria: All but one of the 53 inhabitants of Thalit are killed by guerrillas.
- April 11 – Fire damages the Turin Cathedral in Italy.
- April 14
  - Fire breaks out in a pilgrim camp on the Plain of Mena, 7 miles (11 km) from Mecca; 343 die.
  - Former S.S. Captain Erich Priebke is retried; on July 22 he is sentenced to 5 years in prison.
- April 16 – Houston socialite Doris Angleton is murdered in her River Oaks home. Her brother-in-law, Roger Angleton, later admits to the crime in his suicide note.

- April 18 – The Red River of the North breaks through dikes and floods Grand Forks, North Dakota, and East Grand Forks, Minnesota, causing US$2 billion in damage.
- April 21 – A Pegasus rocket carries the remains of 24 people into earth orbit, in the first space burial.
- April 22
    - Haouch Khemisti massacre: 93 villagers are killed in Algeria.
    - A 126-day hostage crisis at the residence of the Japanese ambassador in Lima, Peru, ends after government commandos storm and capture the building, rescuing 71 hostages. One hostage dies of a heart attack, 2 soldiers are killed by rebel fire, and all 14 Túpac Amaru rebels are slain.
    - France supports the new transitional government in Zaire, withdrawing its support of Mobutu Sese Seko.
- April 23 – 42 villagers are killed in the Omaria massacre in Algeria.
- April 27 – Andrew Cunanan murders Jeffrey Trail, beginning a murder spree that lasts until July and ends with the murder of fashion designer Gianni Versace.
- April 29
    - The Organization for the Prohibition of Chemical Weapons (OPCW), CWC treaty enters into force.
    - Two trains crash at Hunan, China; 126 are killed.

May

- May 2 – The Labour Party of the United Kingdom returns to power for the first time in 18 years, with Tony Blair becoming Prime Minister, in a landslide majority in the 1997 general election.

- May 3 – Katrina and the Waves win the Eurovision Song Contest 1997 for the UK with "Love Shine a Light", the most successful Eurovision entry ever.
- May 8 – Playhouse Disney launches.
- May 10 – The 7.3 Mw Qayen earthquake shakes eastern Iran with a maximum Mercalli intensity of X (*Extreme*). At least were 1,567 killed and 2,300 were injured.
- May 11 – IBM's Deep Blue defeats Garry Kasparov in the last game of the rematch, the first time a computer beats a chess World champion in a match.
- May 12 – The Russian-Chechen Peace Treaty is signed.
- May 14 – The Star Alliance is formed between Air Canada, Lufthansa, Scandinavian Airlines System, Thai Airways International and United Airlines.
- May 15 – The United States government acknowledges existence of the "Secret War" in Laos (1953–1975) during the Vietnam War, and dedicates the Laos Memorial in honor of Hmong and other "Secret War" veterans.
- May 16
  - President Mobutu Sese Seko is exiled from Zaire.
  - U.S. President Bill Clinton issues a formal apology to the surviving victims of the Tuskegee Study of Untreated Syphilis in the Negro Male and their families.
- May 17 – Troops of Laurent Kabila march into Kinshasa.
- May 22 – Kelly Flinn, the U.S. Air Force's first female bomber pilot certified for combat, accepts a general discharge in order to avoid a court-martial.

- May 23 – Mohammad Khatami wins the 1997 Iranian presidential election and becomes the first Iranian Reformist president.
- May 25
    - French legislative election, 1997 first-round voting.
    - Strom Thurmond becomes the longest-serving member in the history of the United States Senate (41 years and 10 months).
    - A military coup in Sierra Leone replaces President Ahmad Tejan Kabbah with Major Johnny Paul Koroma.
- May 27 – The second-deadliest tornado of the 1990s hits in Jarrell, Texas, killing 27 people.
- May 31 – The 13-kilometer Confederation Bridge, the world's longest bridge spanning ice-covered waters, opens between Prince Edward Island and New Brunswick, Canada.

June

- June 1
    - Socialist Party-led Centre-left coalition won the second-round in 1997 French legislative elections, began with the third Cohabitation (1997-2002).
    - Hugo Banzer wins the Presidential elections in Bolivia.
- June 2 – In Denver, Colorado, Timothy McVeigh is convicted on 15 counts of murder and conspiracy for his role in the 1995 Oklahoma City bombing.
- June 6 – In Lacey Township, New Jersey, high school senior Melissa Drexler kills her newborn baby in a toilet.

- June 7 – A computer user known as "_eci" publishes his Microsoft C source code on a Windows 95 and Windows NT exploit, which later becomes WinNuke. The source code gets wide distribution across the internet, and Microsoft is forced to release a security patch.
- June 8 – A United States Coast Guard helicopter crashes near Humboldt Bay, California; all 4 crewmembers perish.
- June 10 – Khmer Rouge leader Pol Pot orders the killing of his defense chief, Son Sen, and 11 of Sen's family members, before Pol Pot flees his northern stronghold (the news does not reach outside Cambodia for 3 days).
- June 11 – In the United Kingdom, the House of Commons votes for a total ban on handguns.
- June 12 – The United States Department of the Treasury unveils a new $50 bill, meant to be more difficult to counterfeit.
- June 13 – A jury sentences Timothy McVeigh to death for his part in the 1995 Oklahoma City bombing.
- June 16 – About 50 are killed in the Daïat Labguer (M'sila) massacre in Algeria.
- June 19 – The fast food chain McDonald's wins a partial victory in its libel trial, known as the McLibel case, against two environmental campaigners.
- June 22 – Swedish musician Ted Gärdestad commits suicide by jumping in front of a train (he is found dead later that morning).
- June 25
    - A massive eruption of the Soufrière Hills volcano on the island of Montserrat leads to evacuation and eventual abandonment of the capital, Plymouth.

- An unmanned Progress spacecraft collides with the Russian space station Mir.
- June 26 – Bertie Ahern is appointed as the 10th Taoiseach of the Republic of Ireland and Mary Harney is appointed as the 16th, and first female, Tánaiste, after their parties, Fianna Fáil and the Progressive Democrats respectively, win the 1997 General Election.
- June 26 – Bloomsbury Publishing publishes J. K. Rowling's *Harry Potter and the Philosopher's Stone* in London.
- June 27 - Walt Disney Feature Animation's thirty-fifth animated feature *Hercules* is released.

July

- July 1 – The United Kingdom hands sovereignty of Hong Kong to the People's Republic of China.
- July 4 – NASA's Pathfinder space probe lands on the surface of Mars.
- July 5 – In Cambodia, Hun Sen of the Cambodian People's Party overthrows Norodom Ranariddh in a coup.
- July 7 – The Great Flood begins in southern Poland.
- July 8
    - Mayo Clinic researchers warn that the dieting drug "fen-phen" can cause severe heart and lung damage.
    - NATO invites the Czech Republic, Hungary, and Poland to join the alliance in 1999.
- July 10
    - In London, scientists report their DNA analysis findings from a Neanderthal skeleton, which support

the out of Africa theory of human evolution, placing an "African Eve" at 100,000 to 200,000 years ago.
- ○ Miguel Ángel Blanco is kidnapped in Ermua, Spain and murdered by the ETA.
- July 11 – Thailand's worst hotel fire at Pattaya kills 90.
- July 13 – The remains of Che Guevara are returned to Cuba for burial, alongside some of his comrades. Guevara and his comrades were executed on 9 October 1967 in Bolivia.
- July 15 – Spree killer Andrew Cunanan shoots fashion designer Gianni Versace to death outside Versace's Miami residence.
- July 16 – The Dow Jones Industrial Average gains 63.17 to close at 8,038.88. It is the Dow's first close above 8,000. The Dow has doubled its value in 30 months.
- July 17 – The F. W. Woolworth Company closes after 117 years in business.
- July 21 – On her 200th birthday, the fully restored USS *Constitution* (aka "Old Ironsides") sets sail for the first time in 116 years.
  - ○ The first genetically modified 3 parent baby is born.
- July 23 – Digital Equipment Corporation files antitrust charges against chipmaker Intel.
- July 24 – Spree killer Andrew Cunanan commits suicide in a Miami houseboat.
- July 25 – K. R. Narayanan is sworn in as India's 10th president and the first member of the Dalit caste to hold this office.
- July 27 – About 50 are killed in the Si Zerrouk massacre in Algeria.

- July 30 – 18 people are killed in the Thredbo landslide in the Snowy Mountains resort in Australia. Stuart Diver is the only survivor.

August

- August 1
  - Boeing and McDonnell Douglas complete a merger.
  - Steve Jobs returns to Apple Computer, Inc at Macworld in Boston.
- August 2 – Australian ski instructor Stuart Diver is rescued as the sole survivor from the Thredbo landslide in New South Wales, in which 18 die.
- August 3 – Between 40–76 villagers are killed in the Oued El-Had and Mezouara massacre in Algeria.
- August 3-11 – Two of the three islands of the Union of the Comoros — Anjouan and Mohéli — attempt to succeed to revert to colonial rule by France. It fails when the French government of President Jacques Chirac refuses to recolonize them resulting in the two islands being reintegrated into the Comoros over the next two years.
- August 4
  - 185,000 Teamsters Union United Parcel Service drivers walk off the job.
  - Jeanne Calment, the oldest person ever, dies at age 122 years 164 days in Arles, France.
- August 6
  - Microsoft buys a $150 million share of financially troubled Apple Computer.

- o Korean Air Flight 801 crash lands west of Guam International Airport, resulting in the deaths of 228 people.
- August 13
  - o In Belo Horizonte, Brazil, Cruzeiro defeats Sporting Cristal of Peru 1–0, becoming the Copa Libertadores de América champions for the second time.
  - o The controversial animated sitcom *South Park* debuts on Comedy Channel.
- August 20 – Over 60 are killed, 15 kidnapped in the Souhane massacre in Algeria.
- August 21 – *Be Here Now*, the third album from English rock band Oasis, becomes the fastest selling album in UK history.
- August 26
  - o 60–100 are killed in the Beni Ali massacre in Algeria.
  - o The Independent International Commission on Decommissioning is set up in Northern Ireland, as part of a peace process.
- August 29 – Over 98 (and possibly up to 400) are killed in the Rais massacre in Algeria.
- August 31 – Death of Diana, Princess of Wales: Diana, Princess of Wales is taken to a hospital after a car accident shortly after midnight, in the Pont de l'Alma road tunnel in Paris. She is pronounced dead at 3:00 am.

September

The funeral cortege of Diana, Princess of Wales, en route to Westminster Abbey from Kensington Palace.

- September 4 – In Lorain, Ohio, the last Ford Thunderbird for 3 years rolls off the assembly line.
- September 5
  - Over 87 are killed in the Beni Messous massacre in Algeria.
  - The International Olympic Committee picks Athens, Greece, to be the host city for the 2004 Summer Olympics.
- September 6
  - The funeral of Diana, Princess of Wales, takes place at Westminster Abbey, watched by over 2 billion people worldwide.
  - A Jean Michel Jarre Oxygene in Moscow concert, celebrating the city's 850th anniversary, draws 3.5 million people.
- September 7 – The F-22 Raptor makes its first test flight.
- September 11 – Scotland votes to create its own Parliament after 290 years of union with England.
- September 13 – Iraq disarmament crisis: An Iraqi military officer attacks an UNSCOM weapons inspector on board an

UNSCOM helicopter, while the inspector attempts to take photographs of unauthorized movement of Iraqi vehicles inside a site designated for inspection.

- September 15 – Norwegian parliamentary election, 1997.
- September 17 – Iraq disarmament crisis: While waiting for access to a site, UNSCOM inspectors witness and videotape Iraqi guards moving files, burning documents, and dumping waste cans into a nearby river.
- September 18
    - Wales votes in favour of devolution and the formation of a National Assembly for Wales.
    - Al-Qaeda carries out a terrorist attack in Mostar, Bosnia and Herzegovina.
- September 19 – 53 are killed in the Guelb El-Kebir massacre in Algeria.
- September 21 – The Islamic Salvation Army, the Islamic Salvation Fronts' armed wing, declares a unilateral ceasefire in Algeria.
- September 25 – Iraq disarmament crisis: UNSCOM inspector Dr. Diane Seaman catches several Iraqi men sneaking out the back door of an inspection site, with log books for the creation of prohibited bacteria and chemicals.
- September 26
    - An air crash in Indonesia (likely caused by smoke rising from numerous forest fires in the area) kills 235 people (see Garuda Indonesia Flight 152).
    - An earthquake strikes the Italian regions of Umbria and Marche, causing part of the Basilica of St. Francis at Assisi to collapse.

- September 27 – The Roman Catholic Diocese of Požega in Croatia is founded.

October

- October 1 – Luke Woodham walks into Pearl High School in Pearl, Mississippi, and opens fire, killing 2 girls, after killing his mother earlier that morning.
- October 2 – British scientists Moira Bruce and John Collinge, with their colleagues, independently show that the new variant form of the Creutzfeldt–Jakob disease is the same disease as Bovine spongiform encephalopathy.
- October 4
  - One million men gather for Promise Keepers' "Stand in the Gap" event in Washington, D.C..
  - Loomis Fargo Bank Robbery: The second largest cash robbery in U.S. history ($17.3 million, mostly in small bills) occurs at the Charlotte, North Carolina office of Wells Fargo. An FBI investigation eventually results in 24 convictions and the recovery of approximately 95% of the stolen cash.
- October 11 – The mixed martial arts organization Pride Fighting Championships holds its inaugural event at the Tokyo Dome in Tokyo, Japan. In the main event Rickson Gracie defeats Nobuhiko Takada by armbar.
- October 12 – 43 are killed at a false roadblock, in the Sidi Daoud massacre in Algeria.
- October 15
  - Andy Green sets the first supersonic land speed record for the ThrustSSC team, led by Richard Noble of the

UK. ThrustSSC goes through the flying mile course at Black Rock Desert, Nevada at an average speed of 1,227.985 km/h (763.035 mph).

- ○ NASA launches the Cassini–Huygens probe to Saturn.
- October 16 – The first color photograph appears on the front page of *The New York Times*.
- October 17 – The remains of Che Guevara are laid to rest with full military honours in a specially built mausoleum in the city of Santa Clara, Cuba, where he had won the decisive battle of the Cuban Revolution 39 years before.
- October 27 – In the U.S., the Dow Jones Industrial Average drops -554.26 points (-7.18%), closing at 7,161.14.
- October 28 – In the U.S., the Dow Jones Industrial Average gains a record 337.17 points (+4.71%), closing at 7,498.32. One billion shares are traded on the New York Stock Exchange for the first time ever.
- October 29 – Iraq disarmament crisis: Iraq says it will begin shooting down Lockheed U-2 surveillance planes being used by UNSCOM inspectors.
- October 30 – In Newton, Massachusetts, British au pair Louise Woodward is found guilty of the baby-shaking death of 8-month-old Matthew Eappen.

November

Mary McAleese

- November 3 – In France, striking truck drivers blockade ports during a pay dispute.
- November 10
  - Telecom companies WorldCom and MCI Communications announce a US$37 billion merger to form MCI WorldCom (the largest merger in U.S. history).
  - A Fairfax, Virginia jury finds Mir Aimal Kasi guilty of murdering 2 CIA employees in 1993.
- November 11 – Mary McAleese is elected the 8th President of Ireland in succession to Mary Robinson, the first time in the world that one woman has succeeded another as elected head of state.
- November 12 – Ramzi Yousef is found guilty of masterminding the 1993 World Trade Center bombing.
- November 17 – In Luxor, Egypt, 62 people are killed by 6 Islamic militants outside the Temple of Hatshepsut.
- November 19 – In Des Moines, Iowa, Bobbi McCaughey gives birth to septuplets in the second known case where all

7 babies are born alive, and the first in which all survive infancy.
- November 27 – NASA's Tropical Rainfall Measuring Mission is launched, the start of the satellite component of the Clouds and the Earth's Radiant Energy System.

December

- December 1 – In the Indian state of Bihar, Ranvir Sena attacks the CPI(ML) Party Unity stronghold Lakshmanpur-Bathe, killing 63 lower caste people.
- December 3 – In Ottawa, Canada, representatives from 121 countries sign a treaty prohibiting the manufacture and deployment of anti-personnel land mines. However, the United States, the People's Republic of China, Russia, South Korea and 32 other nations do not sign and/or ratify the treaty.
- December 8 – Myra Hindley, one of the Moors murderers, arrives at the High Court of Justice, to contest a recent Home Secretary's decision that she should remain in prison until she dies.
- December 10 – The capital of Kazakhstan is moved from Almaty to Astana.
- December 11 – The Kyoto Protocol is adopted by a United Nations committee.
- December 12
  - Demonstrations occur in the state capitals of Australia against the WTO and IMF.
  - The 1997 FIFA Confederations Cup begins in Saudi Arabia.

- December 16 – "Dennō Senshi Porygon", an episode of the Pokémon TV series, is aired in Japan, inducing seizures in hundreds of Japanese children.
- December 18 – Myra Hindley loses her High Court appeal against the government's decision to keep her behind bars for the rest of her life.
- December 19
    - Janet Jagan (the former wife of Cheddi Jagan) takes office in Guyana.
    - James Cameron's *Titanic*, the then highest-grossing film of all time, premieres in the U.S.
- December 21 – Brazil beats Australia 6–0 in the Confederations Cup final.
- December 24 – 50–100 villagers are killed in the Sid El-Antri massacre in Algeria.
- December 27 – Ulster loyalist paramilitary leader Billy Wright is assassinated in Northern Ireland, inside Long Kesh prison.
- December 29 – Hong Kong begins to kill all the chickens within its territory (1.25 million) to stop the spread of a potentially deadly influenza strain.
- December 30 – Wilaya of Relizane massacres of December 30, 1997: In the worst incident in Algeria's insurgency, 400 are killed from four villages in the *wilaya* of Relizane.

Date unknown

- The Toyota Prius, the first hybrid vehicle to go into full production, is unveiled in Japan on October 24, and goes on sale in Japan on December 9. It comes to U.S. showrooms on July 11, 2000.

Births

January

Jack Andraka

Cody Simpson

Nastya and Masha Tolmacheva

Gedion Zelalem

- January 1 – Quique Fornos, Spanish footballer
- January 3 – Joe Morrell, Welsh footballer
- January 4
    - Răzvan Popa, Romanian footballer
    - Carmen LoPorto, American actor
- January 5 – Hilary Palma, Peruvian volleyball player
- January 6 – Vasileios Charalampopoulos, Greek basketball player
- January 7 – Isaiah Brown, English footballer
- January 8
    - Jack Andraka, American scientist
    - Fran Brodić, Croatian footballer

- January 11 – Cody Simpson, Australian singer-songwriter
- January 13
  - José Manuel García Maurin, Spanish footballer
  - Connor McDavid, Canadian ice hockey player
- January 14
  - Nastya and Masha Tolmacheva, Russian singers
  - Joey Luthman, American actor
  - Julius Nättinen, Finnish ice hockey player
  - Francesco Bagnaia, Italian motorcycle racer
- January 17
  - Jack Vidgen, Australian singer
  - Kim Ga-eul, South Korean swimmer
- January 18 – Amber Lily, American singer
- January 20 – Rheed McCracken, Australian wheelchair racer
- January 21 – Yang Yang, Chinese paralympic swimmer
- January 23
  - Gudaf Tsegay, Ethiopian middle-distance runner
  - Joseph and Luka Banda, Zambian formerly conjoined twins
  - Sophie Hahn, English paralympic sprinter
  - Shaheen Jafargholi, Iranian-Welsh actor and singer
  - Lexie Priessman, American artistic gymnast
  - Giorgio Rasulo, English footballer
- January 24 – Dylan Riley Snyder, American actor
- January 26 – Gedion Zelalem, German-American footballer
- January 29 – Melissa Juratowitch, Australian model
- January 30
  - Alexandra Rodriguez Long, Spanish pair skater
  - Shim Suk-hee, South Korean speed skater
- January 31

- ○ Lane Sutton, American entrepreneur
- ○ Eva Sayer, English actress

February

Chloë Grace Moretz

Isabelle Fuhrman

- February 2 – Jaheel Hyde, Jamaican sprinter
- February 3 – Wang Wenting, Chinese pair skater
- February 5
  - ○ Patrick Roberts, English footballer
  - ○ Nicolas Roy, Canadian ice hockey player
- February 7

- Jessica Waterhouse, Australian footballer
- Anhelina Kalinina, Ukrainian tennis player
- February 8
  - Kathryn Newton, American actress
  - Venus Palermo, English model
- February 9 – Molly Jepson, American actress
- February 10
  - Adam Armstrong, English footballer
  - Chloë Grace Moretz, American actress
  - Lauren Mote, English actress
  - Rozaliya Nasretdinova, Russian swimmer
- February 12
  - Matteo Ferrari, Italian motorcycle racer
  - Nikolas Špalek, Slovak footballer
- February 14 – Breel Embolo, Swiss footballer
- February 16 – Charlie Green, English-Filipino singer
- February 20 – Mitchie Brusco, American professional skateboarder
- February 21 – Ben Rhodes, American racing driver
- February 22 – Shaalin Zoya, Indian actress
- February 25
  - Isabelle Fuhrman, American actress
  - Katsiaryna Halkina, Belarusian rhythmic gymnast
  - Anna Koblencová, Czech slalom canoeist

March

Daniel De Silva

Belinda Bencic

Ciara Bravo

Rūta Meilutytė

Martina Stoessel

- March 2
    - Babar Iqbal, Pakistani computer programmer
    - Becky G, American singer
- March 3
    - Infanta Maria Francisca of Portugal
    - Ty Walker, American snowboarder
- March 6 – Daniel De Silva, Australian footballer
- March 8
    - Iréne Ekelund, Swedish sprinter
    - Jurina Matsui, Japanese singer

- March 9
  - Jessica Rogers, American wheelchair athlete
  - Darsheel Safary, Indian actor
  - Niamh Wilson, Canadian actress
- March 10
  - Julia Barretto, Filipina actress
  - Belinda Bencic, Swiss tennis player
  - Travis Konecny, Canadian ice hockey player
- March 11 – Lina Qostal, Moroccan tennis player
- March 12 – Allan Saint-Maximin, French footballer
- March 14
  - Dawid Kownacki, Polish footballer
  - Brad Taylor, English cricketer
- March 16 – Tyrel Jackson Williams, American actor
- March 17 – Katie Ledecky, American swimmer
- March 18 – Ciara Bravo, American actress, voice artist, singer, and comedian
- March 19
  - Rūta Meilutytė, Lithuanian swimmer
  - Kwak Dong-yeon, South Korean actor and singer
- March 20 – Bobby Cheng, Australian chess champion
- March 21 – Martina Stoessel, Argentine actress, singer, dancer and model
- March 22
  - Harry Wilson, Welsh footballer
  - María Fernanda Herazo, Colombian tennis player
- March 23 – Aidan Davis, English street dancer
- March 24 – George Thomas, Welsh footballer
- March 27
  - Princess Aisha bint Al Faisal of Jordan

- Princess Sara bint Al Faisal of Jordan
- March 29
  - Robert Vâlceanu, Romanian footballer
  - Ayesha Norrie, Australian footballer

April

Maisie Williams

Alexander Zverev

Lydia Ko

- April 1
    - Asa Butterfield, English actor
    - Olivia Smart, English ice dancer
- April 4 – Josefine Ridell, Swedish singer
- April 6 – Pavel Zacha, Czech ice hockey player
- April 7
    - Rafaela Gómez, Ecuadorian tennis player
    - Laura van der Heijden, English cellist
- April 8
    - Matthildur Þorsteinsdóttir, Icelandic paralympic long jumper
    - Sayantan Das, Indian chess champion
- April 9 – Michael Špaček, Czech ice hockey player
- April 10– Alla Sosnitskaya, Russian artistic gymnast
- April 11
    - Ethan Couch, American criminal
    - Max Clegg, English speedway racer
- April 12
    - Jacob Clemente, American actor

- Katelyn Ohashi, American artistic gymnast
- April 15
  - Maisie Williams, English actress
  - Jesse Little, American stock car racing driver
- April 16 – Raghav Sood, Indian computer programmer
- April 19 – Alejandra Orozco, Mexican diver
- April 20 – Alexander Zverev, German tennis player
- April 21 – Akanksha Sharma, Indian singer
- April 23
  - Kim Hae-jin, South Korean figure skater
  - Kouta Jige, Hong Kong footballer
- April 24
  - Lydia Ko, South Korean-born New Zealand golfer
  - Arturo Deliser, Panamanian sprinter
  - Veronika Kudermetova, Russian tennis player
- April 25 – Benjamín Inostroza, Chilean footballer
- April 27 – Livio Loi, Belgian motorcycle racer
- April 29 – Ekaterina Baturina, Russian artistic gymnast
- April 30 – Ian Thomas, Belgian musician

May

Ivana Jorović

Odeya Rush

Jake Short

- May 1 – Ariel Gade, American actress
- May 2 – BamBam (singer), a member of South Korean boy group Got7
- May 3 – Ivana Jorović, Serbian tennis player
- May 4 – Gary Lavery, Northern Irish footballer
- May 7
  - Magdalena Klatka, Polish pair skater
  - Youri Tielemans, Belgian footballer
- May 9 – Zane Huett, American actor
- May 10 – Enes Ünal, Turkish footballer

- May 11 – Olivia Tjandramulia, Australian tennis player
- May 12
  - Morgan Lake, English athlete
  - Odeya Rush, Israeli-born American actress
- May 16 – Cloe and Holly Mackie, English actresses
- May 17 – Ayron Verkindere, Belgian footballer
- May 19 – Oliver Kylington, Swedish ice hockey player
- May 21 – Viktoria Petryk, Ukrainian singer-songwriter
- May 23 – Joe Gomez, English footballer
- May 24 – Putri Ayu Silaen, Indonesian singer
- May 26 – Julian Zhi Jie Yee, Malaysian figure skater
- May 27 – Kenneth Weishuhn, American gay bullying victim (d. 2012)
- May 28 – Maguilaura Frias, Peruvian volleyball player
- May 30 – Jake Short, American actor
- May 31 – Inês Murta, Portuguese tennis player

June

Mary-Lynn Neil

- June 2 – Roxana Popa, Spanish artistic gymnast
- June 4

- ○ Kana Nakanishi, Japanese singer
- ○ Carina Lorenzo, Dominican handball player
- ○ Riho, Japanese professional wrestler
- June 8 – Jeļena Ostapenko, Latvian tennis player
- June 9 – Shen Duo, Chinese swimmer
- June 10
  - ○ Sviatoslav Mykhailiuk, Ukrainian basketball player
  - ○ Fletcher O'Leary, Australian actor
- June 11
  - ○ Julia Lavrentieva, Ukrainian pair skater
  - ○ John Hunter Nemechek, American stock car racing driver
- June 12 – Gabrielle Jupp, British artistic gymnast
- June 15 – Madison Kocian, American artistic gymnast
- June 18 – Mary-Lynn Neil, Canadian singer-songwriter
- June 20
  - ○ Maria Lark, Russian-born American actress
  - ○ Giuseppe Bausilio, Swiss actor
- June 21
  - ○ Ferdinand Zvonimir von Habsburg, Austrian head of the royal House of Habsburg-Lorraine
  - ○ Rebecca Black, American singer
- June 27 – Felix Dean, Australian actor
- June 30
  - ○ Avika Gor, Indian actress
  - ○ Iryna Shymanovich, Russian tennis player

July

Grigoriy Oparin

Malala Yousafzai

Chiara Hölzl

- July 1 – Grigoriy Oparin, Russian chess Grandmaster

- July 2 – İbrahim Halil Keser, Turkish footballer
- July 3
    - Mia McKenna-Bruce, English actress
    - Georgios Papagiannis, Greek basketball player
    - Filip Sachpekidis, Swedish footballer
- July 4 – Jason Spevack, Canadian actor
- July 5
    - Park Ji-min, South Korean singer
    - Anna Styazhkina, Russian chess champion
- July 7 – Erina Ikuta, Japanese singer
- July 8 – Bryce Love, American sprinter
- July 10 – Rena Kato, Japanese singer
- July 12 – Malala Yousafzai, Pakistani activist and Nobel Peace Prize laureate
- July 13 – Leo Howard, American actor and martial artist
- July 15 – Phathana Inthavong, Laotian swimmer
- July 17
    - Hardy Binguila, Congolese footballer
    - Sadie Robertson, American television personality
- July 18
    - Chiara Hölzl, Austrian ski jumper
    - Kwon Jin-ah, South Korean singer
- July 19 – Kang Young-seo, South Korean alpine skier
- July 22 – Fergus Riordan, British actor
- July 24 – Andreas Varady, Slovak jazz guitarist
- July 25
    - Kayli Barker, American race car driver
    - Louis Reed, English footballer
- July 27 – Craig Wighton, Scottish footballer
- July 28 – Bilal Ould-Chikh, Dutch-Moroccan footballer

- July 30 – Steven Purugganan, American sport stacker
- July 31 – Barbie Forteza, Filipina actress

August

Daniel Crowley

Olivia Holt

Kylie Jenner

- August 2
  - Christina Robinson, American actress
  - Ivan Šaponjić, Serbian footballer
- August 3 – Daniel Crowley, English footballer
- August 4
  - Ekaterina Ryabova, Russian singer
  - Cinzia Zehnder, Swiss footballer
- August 5
  - Olivia Holt, American actress
  - Adam Irigoyen, American actor
  - Xu Jiao, Chinese actress
  - Laura Waem, Belgian artistic gymnast
  - Clara van Wel, English-born New Zealand singer, songwriter
- August 6 – Sander Svendsen, Norwegian footballer
- August 10 – Kylie Jenner, American model and television personality
- August 13 – Yeo Jin-goo, South Korean actor
- August 14 – Łukasz Pawlikowski, Polish cellist
- August 16 – Greyson Chance, American singer, songwriter and actor
- August 19
  - Joseph Castanon, American actor
  - Maria Titova, Russian rhythmic gymnast
- August 22 – Neil O'Brien, Irish actor
- August 24
  - Betül Taygar, Turkish ice hockey player
  - Alan Walker, Norwegian music producer
- August 26 – Lisa, French singer
- August 30 – Dana Gaier, American actress

September

Tsukushi

Max Verstappen

- September 1 – Maria Stavitskaia, Russian figure skater
- September 3
  - Tatiana Tudvaseva, Russian pair skater
  - Salome Phajava, Georgian rhythmic gymnast
- September 6 – Tsukushi, Japanese professional wrestler
- September 9 – Shriya Sharma, Indian actress
- September 13 – Leah Keiser, American figure skater
- September 14
  - Pragathi Guruprasad, Indian playback singer
  - Benjamin Wahlgren Ingrosso, Swedish singer and actor

- September 16
  - Zsanett Kaján, Hungarian footballer
  - Julian Marcus Trono, Filipino actor
- September 18 – Alisson Krystle Perticheto, Filipina figure skater
- September 20 – Aurélie Fanchette, Seychellois swimmer
- September 24 – Malaya Watson, American singer and tuba player
- September 29 – Luara Hayrapetyan, Armenian singer-songwriter
- September 30
  - Yana Kudryavtseva, Russian rhythmic gymnast
  - Max Verstappen, Dutch racing driver

October

Bella Thorne

- October 2 – Justina Sharp, American fashion blogger
- October 3 – Jin Boyang, Chinese figure skater
- October 4 – Seamus O'Connor, Irish snowboarder
- October 6 – Chih-I Tsao, Taiwanese figure skater
- October 7 – Kira Kosarin, American actress
- October 8 – Bella Thorne, American actress

- October 11 – Tathoi Deb, Indian actress
- October 15 – Adora Svitak, American child prodigy
- October 23
    - Daphne Blunt, American fashion blogger
    - Zach Callison, American actor
- October 24
    - Raúl Chávez Sarmiento, Peruvian child prodigy
    - Park So-youn, South Korean figure skater
- October 27 – Li Meiyi, Chinese pair skater
- October 28 – Sierra McCormick, American actress
- October 31 – Sydney Park, American actress and comedian

November

Stratos Iordanoglou

James Whitley

- November 1 – Alex Wolff, American singer-songwriter, musician, and actor
- November 3 – Lázaro Martínez, Cuban triple jumper
- November 4
  - Stratos Iordanoglou, Greek basketball player
  - Sandra Samir, Egyptian tennis player
- November 6 – Hero Fiennes-Tiffin, English actor
- November 7 – Martina Piemonte, Italian footballer
- November 9 – Matthew Fisher, English cricketer
- November 10 – Khalil Madovi, English rapper and actor
- November 13 – Brent and Shane Kinsman, American actors
- November 17 – James Whitley, British paralympic skier
- November 19
  - Kenny, Alexis, Natalie, Kelsey, Nathan, Brandon and Joel McCaughey, American citizens, first set of septuplets to survive infancy
  - Maud Chifamba, Zimbabwean citizen, youngest university student in Africa
  - Rachel Parsons, American ice dancer
- November 23 – Akari Takeuchi, Japanese singer
- November 27 – Song Yoo-geun, South Korean child prodigy, youngest university student in the country
- November 28 – Thor Salden, Belgian singer
- November 29
  - Agata Kryger, Polish figure skater
  - Ye Qiuyu, Chinese tennis player
- November 30 – Liu Huixia, Chinese diver

December

Ana Konjuh

- December 3 – Hayley Okines, English progeria activist (d. 2015)
- December 4 – Ruru Madrid, Filipino actor
- December 8 – Ilaria Käslin, Swiss artistic gymnast
- December 11 – Ben Cook, American actor
- December 15
  - Stefania LaVie Owen, American-New Zealand actress
  - Magdalena Fręch, Polish tennis player
- December 16 – Zara Larsson, Swedish singer
- December 17 – Shoma Uno, Japanese figure skater
- December 18 – Jeremy Fernandez, American singer
- December 20 – Suzuka Nakamoto, Japanese singer (Babymetal)
- December 24 – Oreoluwa Cherebin, Grenadian swimmer
- December 27
  - Ana Konjuh, Croatian tennis player
  - Zhao Ziquan, Chinese figure skater
- December 30 – Anastasiya Malyavina, Ukrainian swimmer

Deaths

January

Melvin Calvin

- January 1 – Townes Van Zandt, American folk singer (b. 1944)
- January 4 – Harry Helmsley, American real estate mogul (b. 1909)
- January 5 – Burton Lane, American composer and lyricist (b. 1912)
- January 6 – Catherine Scorsese, Italian-American actress (b. 1912)
- January 8 – Melvin Calvin, American chemist (b. 1911)
- January 9 – Jesse White, American actor (b. 1917)
- January 10
  - Sheldon Leonard, American producer, actor, director (b. 1907)
  - Alexander R. Todd, Baron Todd, Scottish chemist, Nobel Prize laureate (b. 1907)
- January 12

- Charles Brenton Huggins, Canadian-born cancer researcher, recipient of the Nobel Prize in Physiology or Medicine (b. 1901)
- Jill Summers, English actress (b. 1910)
- January 17 – Clyde Tombaugh, American astronomer (b. 1906)
- January 18 – Paul Tsongas, U.S. Senator from Massachusetts and one-time candidate for the Democratic presidential nomination (b. 1941)
- January 19
  - James Dickey, American poet and novelist (b. 1923)
  - Adriana Caselotti, American actress (b. 1916)
- January 20
  - Curt Flood, American baseball player (b. 1938)
  - Edith Brown, one of the last remaining and oldest survivors of the sinking of the RMS Titanic in April 1912 (b. 1896)
- January 21
  - Colonel Tom Parker, Dutch-born celebrity manager (b. 1909)
  - Pilar Barbosa, Puerto Rican educator and historian (b. 1898)
- January 22 – Billy Mackenzie, Scottish singer (b. 1957)
- January 23 – Richard Berry African-American singer and composer (b. 1935)
- January 24 - Gengan Tonaki Japan's oldest living man (b. 1884)
- January 25 – Jeane Dixon, American astrologer (b. 1904)

- January 27 – Cecil Arthur Lewis MC, British fighter pilot who flew in World War I and last surviving World War I ace (b. 1898)
- January 30 – Charles Hargens, American painter. (b. 1893)
- January 31 – Johnny Klein, American drummer (b. 1918)

February

Deng Xiaoping

- February 1
  - Herb Caen, American newspaper columnist (b. 1916)
  - Marjorie Reynolds, American actress (b. 1917)
- February 2 – Chico Science, Brazilian musician (b. 1967)
- February 5 – Pamela Harriman, U.S. Ambassador to France (b. 1920)
- February 8 – Corey Scott, American motorcycle stunt rider (b. 1968)
- February 9
  - Brian Connolly, Scottish musician (b. 1945)
  - Barry Evans, English actor (b. 1943)
- February 11 – Don Porter, American actor (b. 1912)
- February 12 – James Cossins, English actor (b. 1933)
- February 13 – John Ries Bartels, United States federal judge (b. 1897)

- February 15 – Luras,Giovanni Giua Italian engineer and officer (b. 1895)
- February 16 – Ethel Owen, American actress (b. 1893)
- February 17
  - Zein Isa, Palestinian militant imprisoned in the United States for the honor killing of his daughter
  - Henry Jacques Le Même, French architect (b. 1897)
  - Nic Roeser, Luxembourgian gymnast who competed at the 1928 Summer Olympics (b. 1896)
- February 19 – Deng Xiaoping, leader of the People's Republic of China (b. 1904)
- February 23 – Tony Williams, American musician (b. 1945)
- February 24 – Isabelle Lucas, Canadian-born British actress (b. 1927)
- February 26 – David Doyle, American actor (b. 1929)

March

Friedrich Hund

- March 4
  - Robert H. Dicke, American experimental physicist (b. 1916)
  - Carey Loftin, American actor and stuntman (b. 1914)

- March 6
    - Cheddi Jagan, President of Guyana (b. 1918)
    - Ursula Torday, British writer (b. 1912)
- March 7
    - Edward Mills Purcell, American physicist, Nobel Prize laureate (b. 1912)
    - Martin Kippenberger, German artist (b. 1953)
- March 9
    - The Notorious B.I.G., American rapper (b. 1972)
    - Terry Nation, Welsh screenwriter (b. 1930)
- March 10 – LaVern Baker, American singer (b. 1929)
- March 14 – Fred Zinnemann, Austrian-born director (b. 1907)
- March 15 – Gail Davis, American actress (b. 1925)
- March 17 – Jermaine Stewart, American singer (b. 1957)
- March 19 – Willem de Kooning, Dutch artist (b. 1904)
- March 20 – Tony Zale, American boxer (b. 1913)
- March 21
    - Wilbert Awdry, British children's writer (b. 1911)
    - John Nemechek, NASCAR driver (b. 1970)
- March 31 – Friedrich Hund, American physics (b. 1896)

April

Allen Ginsberg

- April 1 – Jolie Gabor, Hungarian socialite (b. 1896)
- April 4 – Leo Picard, Israeli geologist and an expert in the field of hydrology (b. 1900)
- April 5
    - Allen Ginsberg, American poet (b. 1926)
    - Ignazio Buttitta, Sicilian dialectal poet (b. 1899)
- April 8 – Laura Nyro, American singer and composer (b. 1947)
- April 7
    - Witto Aloma, Cuban baseball player (b. 1923)
    - Georgy Shonin, Russian cosmonaut (b. 1935)
- April 12 – George Wald, American scientist, recipient of the Nobel Prize in Physiology or Medicine (b. 1906)
- April 13
    - Dorothy Frooks, American author, publisher, military figure and actress. (b. 1896)
    - Rodolfo Oroz, Chilean writer, professor, and philologist,won the Chilean National Prize for Literature in 1978. (b. 1895)
- April 15 – Mildred Cleghorn, Chairwoman of the Fort Sill Apache tribe (b. 1910)
- April 16
    - Doris Angleton, American socialite (b. 1951)
    - Roland Topor, French illustrator (b. 1938)
- April 19 – El Duce, American singer and drummer (b. 1958)
- April 20
    - Jean Louis, American costume designer (b. 1907)
    - Henry Mucci, American Colonel of the 98th Ranger Battalion (b. 1909)

- April 21 – Diosdado Macapagal, 9th President of the Philippines (b. 1910)
- April 22
    - Reg Gammon, English painter and illustrator (b. 1894)
    - Baroness Seear, President of the UK Liberal Party (b. 1913)
- April 24 – Pat Paulsen, American comedian (b. 1927)
- April 26 – John Beal, American actor (b. 1909)
- April 30 – Henry Picard, American golfer (b. 1906)

May

Manfred von Ardenne

- May 1 – Bo Widerberg, Swedish film director (b. 1930)
- May 2 – John Eccles, Australian neurophysiologist, recipient of the Nobel Prize in Physiology or Medicine (b. 1903)
- May 4 – Alvy Moore, American actor (b. 1921)
- May 5 – Walter Gotell, German actor (b. 1924)
- May 11 – Howard Morton, American actor (b. 1925)
- May 14
    - Harry Blackstone Jr., American magician (b. 1934)
    - Thelma Carpenter, American singer and actress (b. 1922)
- May 16 – Giuseppe De Santis, Italian film director (b. 1917)

- ○ May 22
- ○ Alfred Hershey, American biochemist, recipient of the Nobel Prize in Physiology or Medicine (b. 1908)
- ○ Stanisław Swianiewicz, Polish economist and historian. (b. 1899)
- May 23 – James Lee Byars, American artist (b. 1932)
- May 24 – Edward Mulhare, Irish actor (b. 1923)
- May 26
  - ○ Manfred von Ardenne, German research and applied physicist and inventor. (b. 1907)
  - ○ Ralph Horween, American football player and coach. (b. 1896)
- May 29
  - ○ Jeff Buckley, American musician (b. 1966)
  - ○ George Fenneman, American radio and television announcer (b. 1919)
- May 31 – James Bennett Griffin, American archaeologist (b. 1905)

June

Jacques-Yves Cousteau

- June 2 – Helen Jacobs, American tennis champion (b. 1908)
- June 3 – Dennis James, American game show host (b. 1917)

- June 6 – Magda Gabor, American actress (b. 1914)
- June 8 – Reid Shelton, American actor (b. 1924)
- June 12 – Bulat Okudzhava, Soviet non-mainstream singer of Georgian descent (b. 1924)
- June 14
  - Helmut Fischer, German actor (b. 1926)
  - Richard Jaeckel, American actor (b. 1926)
- June 15 – Jaidyn Leskie, Australian murder victim (b. 1996)
- June 22
  - Gérard Pelletier, French journalist, politician and diplomat (b. 1919)
  - Don Henderson, British actor (b. 1932)
- June 23
  - Betty Shabazz, American widow of Malcolm X (b. 1936)
  - William Slater Brown, American novelist, biographer and translator of French literature (b. 1896)
- June 24
  - Don Hutson, American football player (b. 1913)
  - Brian Keith, American actor (b. 1921)
- June 25 – Jacques-Yves Cousteau, French explorer (b. 1910)
- June 26 – Israel Kamakawiwo'ole, Hawaiian singer (b. 1959)
- June 28 – Mrs. Miller, American singer (b. 1907)
- June 29 – William Hickey, American actor (b. 1927)

July

Robert Mitchum

James Stewart

Gianni Versace

- July 1
    - Robert Mitchum, American actor (b. 1917)
    - Charles Werner, American cartoonist (b. 1909)
- July 2 – James Stewart, American actor (b. 1908)
- July 4
    - Charles Kuralt, American television reporter (b. 1934)
    - John Zachary Young, British biologist (b. 1907)
- July 7 – Royston Tickner, English actor (b. 1922)
- July 13 – Alexandra Danilova, Russian dancer (b. 1903)
- July 14 – Sir Garfield Barwick, Australian Chief Justice (b. 1903)
- July 15 – Gianni Versace, Italian fashion designer (b. 1946)
- July 18 – Eugene Merle Shoemaker, American astronomer (b. 1928)
- July 20 – John Akii-Bua Ugandan hurdler (b. 1949)

- July 23 – Chūhei Nambu, Japanese athlete (b. 1904)
- July 24
  - William J. Brennan, U.S. Supreme Court Justice (b. 1906)
  - Frank Parker, American tennis champion (b. 1916)
- July 25 – Ben Hogan, American golf champion (b. 1912)
- July 27 – K'tut Tantri, broadcaster/hotelier, (b. 1899)
- July 30 – Bảo Đại, Emperor of Vietnam (b. 1913)

August

Jeanne Calment

Diana, Princess of Wales

- August 1
  - Sviatoslav Richter, Ukrainian pianist (b. 1915)
- August 2

- William S. Burroughs, American author (b. 1914)
  - Fela Kuti, Nigerian musician and political activist (b. 1938)
- August 4 – Jeanne Calment, French supercentenarian and the oldest living person ever documented in history. (b. 1875)
- August 10 – Conlon Nancarrow, American-born composer (b. 1912)
- August 12 – Luther Allison, American musician (b. 1939)
- August 16 – Nusrat Fateh Ali Khan, Pakistani *Qawwali* musician (b. 1948)
- August 18 – Harry R. Wellman, University of California president (b. 1899)
- August 21 – Yuri Nikulin, Soviet and Russian actor and clown (b. 1921)
- August 23 – John Kendrew, British molecular biologist, recipient of the Nobel Prize in Chemistry (b. 1917)
- August 24 – Louis Essen, English physicist (b. 1908)
- August 27
  - Sally Blane, American actress (b. 1910)
  - Brandon Tartikoff, American television executive (b. 1949)
- August 28 – Masaru Takumi, Japanese yakuza lord (b. 1936)
- August 31
  - Diana, Princess of Wales, British princess and first wife of Charles, Prince of Wales (b. 1961)
  - Dodi Al-Fayed, Egyptian businessman (b. 1955)

September

Mother Teresa

Mobutu Sese Seko

- September 2
  - Rudolf Bing, Austrian opera manager (b. 1902)
  - Viktor Frankl, Austrian neurologist and psychiatrist (b. 1905)
- September 5
  - Georg Solti, Hungarian conductor (b. 1912)
  - Mother Teresa, Albanian missionary, recipient of the Nobel Peace Prize (b. 1910)
- September 7
  - Elisabeth Brooks, Canadian actress (*The Howling*) (b. 1951)
  - Mobutu Sese Seko, president of Zaire (b. 1930)

- September 8 – Helen Shaw, American actress (b. 1897)
- September 9 – Burgess Meredith, American actor (b. 1907)
- September 12 – Leonard Maguire, Scottish actor (b. 1924)
- September 17 – Red Skelton, American comedian (b. 1913)
- September 18 – Jimmy Witherspoon, American blues singer (b. 1920)
- September 19
  - Jack May, English actor (b. 1922)
  - Rich Mullins, American musician (b. 1955)
- September 23
  - Shirley Clarke, American filmmaker (b. 1919)
  - Wilbur R. Ingalls, Jr., American architect (b. 1923)
- September 25 – Jean Françaix, French composer (b. 1912)
- September 27 – Walter Trampler, German violist (b. 1915)
- September 29 – Roy Lichtenstein, American artist (b. 1923)
- September 30 – Milner Gray (designer), British industrial design (b. 1899)

October

Brian Pillman

Audra Lindley

- October 1 – Jerome H. Lemelson, American inventor (b. 1923)
- October 4
  - Otto Ernst Remer, German Wehrmacht officer (b. 1912)
  - Gunpei Yokoi, Japanese video game franchise creator (b. 1941)
- October 5
  - Brian Pillman, American professional wrestler (b. 1962)
  - Arthur Tracy, American singer (b. 1899)
- October 6
  - Adrienne Hill, British actress (b. 1937)
  - Johnny Vander Meer, baseball player (b. 1914)
- October 12 – John Denver, American musician (b. 1943)
- October 13 – Adil Çarçani, Albanian politician, former Prime Minister (b. 1922)
- October 14 – Harold Robbins, American writer (b. 1916)
- October 16
  - Audra Lindley, American actress (b. 1918)
  - James A. Michener, American writer (b. 1907)
- October 19 – Glen Buxton, American guitarist (b. 1947)
- October 20 – Ron Tarr, English actor (b. 1936)
- October 22 – Leonid Amalrik, Russian animator (b. 1905)

- October 23 – Bert Haanstra, Dutch filmmaker (b. 1916)
- October 24 – Don Messick, American voice actor (b. 1926)
- October 25 – Tina Lattanzi, Italian actress and voice actress (b. 1897)
- October 28 – Paul Jarrico, American screenwriter (b. 1915)
- October 29
  - Andreas Gerasimos Michalitsianos, Greek-American NASA astrophysicist (b. 1947)
  - Anton Szandor LaVey, American founder of the Church of Satan (b. 1930)
  - Alexander zu Dohna-Schlobitten (1899–1997),German Junker, soldier, business man and author (b. 1899)
- October 30 – Samuel Fuller, American screenwriter and director (b. 1912)

November

- November 1 – Victor Mills, chemical engineer for the Procter & Gamble company (b. 1897)
- November 5 – George Philip Bradley "Pip" Roberts, British general (b. 1906)
- November 6 – Lillian Rogers Parks, American housemaid and seamstress in the White House. (b. 1897)
- November 8 – Mohammad-Ali Jamalzadeh, one of the most prominent writers of Iran in the 20th century (b. 1892)
- November 11 – Rod Milburn, American athlete (b. 1950)
- November 12 – Carlos Surinach, Spanish composer (b. 1915)
- November 18 – Un'ichi Hiratsuka, Japanese print-maker. (b. 1895)
- November 21 – Robert Simpson, English composer (b. 1921)

- November 22 – Michael Hutchence, Australian singer-songwriter (INXS) (b. 1960)
- November 23 – Hulda Crooks, American mountaineer (b. 1896)
- November 25
    - Monique Serf, French singer (b. 1930)
    - Hastings Kamuzu Banda, former President of Malawi (b. 1898)

December

Stéphane Grappelli

- December 1 – Stéphane Grappelli, French violinist (b. 1908)
- December 2
    - Shirley Crabtree, British wrestler best known as Big Daddy (b. 1930)
    - Michael Hedges, American composer and guitarist (b. 1953)
- December 7 – Billy Bremner, British footballer (b. 1942)
- December 9 – Lucy Jane Askew, British oldest living person.(b. 1883)
- December 14

- o Stubby Kaye, American actor (b. 1918)
- o Owen Barfield, British philosopher, author, poet, and critic (b. 1898)
- December 16
  - o Lillian Disney, the wife of Walt Disney. (b. 1899)
  - o Nicolette Larson, American pop singer (b. 1952)
  - o Thomas J. Parmley, professor at the University of Utah (b. 1897)
- December 18 – Chris Farley, American actor and comedian (b. 1964)
- December 19
  - o Masaru Ibuka, Japanese electronics industrialist, co-founder of Sony (b. 1908)
  - o David Schramm, American astrophysicist (b. 1945)
- December 20
  - o Juzo Itami, Japanese film director (b. 1933)
  - o Denise Levertov, English-born American poet (b. 1923)
- December 21 – Amie Comeaux, American country singer (b. 1976)
- December 23 – Stanley Cortez, American cinematographer (b. 1908)
- December 24 – Toshiro Mifune, Japanese actor (b. 1920)
- December 25
  - o Denver Pyle, American actor (b. 1920)
  - o Anita Conti, French explorer and photographer (b. 1899)
- December 27 – Billy Wright, Northern Irish paramilitary leader (b. 1960)
- December 31
  - o Billie Dove, American actress (b. 1903)

- ○ Michael Kennedy, son of Robert F. Kennedy (b. 1958)

Date unknown

- Laurence Henry Hicks, Australian composer (b. 1912)

Nobel Prizes

- Chemistry – Paul D. Boyer, John E. Walker, Jens C. Skou
- Economics – Bank of Sweden – Robert C. Merton, Myron Scholes
- Literature – Dario Fo
- Peace – International Campaign to Ban Landmines and Jody Williams
- Physics – Steven Chu, Claude Cohen-Tannoudji, William D. Phillips
- Medicine – Stanley B. Prusiner

In the News.

Hong Kong returned to Chinese rule from UK rule.

Diana Princess of Wales is killed in a car crash in Paris.

Princess Diana's funeral watched by 1.5 billion people around the world.

Tony Blair becomes Prime Minister of the United Kingdom.

Mother Teresa Dies in Calcutta.

Mike Tyson Bites Evander Holyfield's ear during a match and is suspended from boxing.

Woolworths closes its remaining discount stores after more than 100 years of trading.

A civil jury panel finds OJ Simpson Guilty.

Tiger Woods at 21 years old became the youngest ever golfer to win the Masters.

The first book in the award winning Harry Potter series by J. K. Rowling is published "Harry Potter and the Philosopher's Stone"

Scientists in Scotland reveal the first successful cloning of an adult mammal a sheep named Dolly.

Popular Films - Titanic, The Lost World: Jurassic Park, Men in Black.

1997 Calendar.

January 1997

Sun	Mon	Tue	Wed	Thu	Fri	Sat
			1	2	3	4
5	6	7	8	9	10	11
12	13	14	15	16	17	18
19	20	21	22	23	24	25
26	27	28	29	30	31	

February 1997

Sun	Mon	Tue	Wed	Thu	Fri	Sat
						1
2	3	4	5	6	7	8
9	10	11	12	13	14	15
16	17	18	19	20	21	22
23	24	25	26	27	28	

March 1997

Sun	Mon	Tue	Wed	Thu	Fri	Sat
						1
2	3	4	5	6	7	8
9	10	11	12	13	14	1
16	17	18	19	20	21	2
23	24	25	26	27	28	2
30	31					

April 1997

Sun	Mon	Tue	Wed	Thu	Fri	Sat
		1	2	3	4	5
6	7	8	9	10	11	12
13	14	15	16	17	18	19
20	21	22	23	24	25	26
27	28	29	30			

May 1997

Sun	Mon	Tue	Wed	Thu	Fri	Sat
				1	2	3
4	5	6	7	8	9	10
11	12	13	14	15	16	17
18	19	20	21	22	23	24
25	26	27	28	29	30	31

June 1997

Sun	Mon	Tue	Wed	Thu	Fri	Sa
1	2	3	4	5	6	7
8	9	10	11	12	13	14
15	16	17	18	19	20	21
22	23	24	25	26	27	28
29	30					

July 1997

Sun	Mon	Tue	Wed	Thu	Fri	Sat
		1	2	3	4	5
6	7	8	9	10	11	12
13	14	15	16	17	18	19
20	21	22	23	24	25	26
27	28	29	30	31		

August 1997

Sun	Mon	Tue	Wed	Thu	Fri	Sat
					1	2
3	4	5	6	7	8	9
10	11	12	13	14	15	16
17	18	19	20	21	22	23
24	25	26	27	28	29	30
31						

September 199

Sun	Mon	Tue	Wed	Thu	Fri	Sa
	1	2	3	4	5	6
7	8	9	10	11	12	13
14	15	16	17	18	19	20
21	22	23	24	25	26	27
28	29	30				

October 1997

Sun	Mon	Tue	Wed	Thu	Fri	Sat
			1	2	3	4
5	6	7	8	9	10	11
12	13	14	15	16	17	18
19	20	21	22	23	24	25
26	27	28	29	30	31	

November 1997

Sun	Mon	Tue	Wed	Thu	Fri	Sat
						1
2	3	4	5	6	7	8
9	10	11	12	13	14	15
16	17	18	19	20	21	22
23	24	25	26	27	28	29
30						

December 1997

Sun	Mon	Tue	Wed	Thu	Fri	Sa
	1	2	3	4	5	6
7	8	9	10	11	12	13
14	15	16	17	18	19	20
21	22	23	24	25	26	27
28	29	30	31